Young Sam Walton
An American Boy
Study Guide

by

Brenda Turner

ISBN: 978-1-949231-87-8
Young Sam Walton An American Boy Study Guide

Yorkshire Publishing
3207 South Norwood Avenue
Tulsa, Oklahoma 74135
www.YorkshirePublishing.com
918.394.2665

TABLE OF CONTENTS

About this Study Guide

Discussion questions, writers connections, and learning extensions are divided into the following sections: On the Farm, Accomplishments, Moves, Jobs, and Rules for Success.

Additional support is given to enrich student learning with biography graphic organizers, vocabulary study, and a setting chart for students to complete.

Students can demonstrate their knowledge of YOUNG SAM WALTON by completing a final biography project from the menu of choices. A rubric is provided for the project.

Two STEM challenges are included that are based on the book. In addition to the challenges, tips and helpful links are included along with additional STEM information for background knowledge.

Brenda Turner is an author and National Board Certified Teacher with a Master's degree in Gifted and Talented Education. She has been an elementary classroom teacher and is currently a Gifted Facilitator for two elementary schools. Brenda enjoys researching to weave historically accurate and creative stories for her readers. She travels extensively, often discovering inspiration for a new project around the next corner.

Contact Brenda at brendaturnerbooks.com.

On the Farm

Discussion Questions:

1. What are chores that Sam helped with on the farm? What are chores you help with in your home?
2. World War I ended on November 11, 1918. What important holiday do we celebrate on this date?

Writers Connection:

We celebrate many freedoms in our country that have been protected by our veterans. Write a thank you letter to a veteran thanking them for their service to our country.

Extensions:

1. Kingfisher was settled as a result of the first Oklahoma Land Run. Have students research the first land rush in Oklahoma that was called Harrison's Horse Race.
2. Life on a farm is different than life in a city. Have students create a Venn Diagram comparing the two.
3. There are many domestic animals found on a farm. Have student select one animal to research and create a brochure explaining how to care for the animal. *(Suggestions: horse, cow, chickens, pig)*
4. World War I was a pivotal event in American History. What does armistice mean? What United States President changed the name of Armistice Day to Veteran's Day? What is special about the number 11 on Veteran's Day? Have students present these facts in a 12x18 poster or digital slideshow. *(Armistice: an agreement to stop fighting at a specific time, a truce. President Dwight D. Eisenhower changed the name. Armistice occurred at the 11th hour on the 11th day of the 11th month in 1918.)*

Accomplishments

Discussion Questions:

1. Sam was determined to be the youngest boy in the state of Missouri to become an Eagle Scout. Why do you think he set this goal?
2. Sam saved his friend, Donald Peterson, from drowning. Why do you think he took action instead of sitting back and watching from the river bank? Have you had a time in your life when you had to take action and not sit back and watch?
3. Sam became a leader on campus at the University of Missouri. What were some of the leadership characteristics Sam had that made others want to elect him to the different offices?

Writers Connection:

Sam was an individual who set goals for himself. What is a goal you want to accomplish? What steps do you need to do to accomplish your goal? Write your goal and the steps to reach it.

Extensions:

1. Have students create a list of at least 15 different badges that can be earned by a Boy Scout.
2. Sam was able to use lifesaving skills he learned as a Boy Scout to save Donald. Have students research the basic steps of CPR and create a chart to show the steps.
3. Sam was an officer in the ROTC. What do the letters stand for? *(Reserve Officers' Training Corp)* What is the purpose of ROTC? *(ROTC is a college program that teaches leadership, military, and career training)*

Moves

Discussion Questions:

1. Sam lived in five towns before graduating from high school. This meant he had to also change schools. How do you think Sam went about making friends?
2. The author paints a picture of how Sam was growing physically by the way he fit in the backseat of the family car. As Sam had to pack and move each time, what do you suppose he was thinking about with the moves?
3. In the book you learn how many miles Sam traveled for each of the moves. How many total miles did Sam travel for the moves? *(650 miles)*

Writers Connection:

Have you had to move before? If so, what did you believe to be the biggest challenge of the move? Write a short story about a move you have made or create a list of what you feel would be the most important items to pack that you own.

Extensions:

1. Sam's family packed the car for each move. Select a car from the 1920s to research like the Ford Model T, Ford Model A or 1924 Chrysler B-70 to research. What did the car cost new? What would the car cost today? Draw a sketch of the car. (inflation calculator: https://www.bls.gov/data/inflation_calculator.htm)
2. Create a map that shows the cities that Sam moved to from Oklahoma to Missouri.

Jobs

Discussion Questions:

1. What do you think of Sam starting to earn money to help his family when he was only in 2nd grade?
2. What job do you think was the most difficult for Sam to do? Why?
3. How did Sam's attitude towards work help him as an adult?

Writers Connection:

Your biggest job right now is to learn while you are in school. How can you work better at your school job? Create a list of how you can improve the way you learn at school.

Extensions:

1. Create a picture collage showing Sam's various jobs from childhood until he opened his Ben Franklin 5 & 10 store in Newport, Arkansas.
2. During his childhood, Sam sold many things. Make a list of the items Sam sold as a child and then look on Walmart.com to see what items Walmart sells today that Sam sold in the past.
3. Of the jobs that Sam worked, which one(s) do you think prepared him to create and build Walmart? Rank the jobs Sam had from what you think is most important to least important.

10 Rules for Success

Discussion Questions:

1. How do you think Sam learned his 10 rules for success?
2. Choose one rule you think is more important than the others and explain why.
3. Do you think there is a reason Sam listed the rules for success in this order?

Writers Connection:

Which rule(s) would be easiest to follow right now? Write the rule and then tell how you will accomplish following it.

Extensions:

1. Many successful individuals have their own rules for success. Read a biography from another individual. Create a Venn Diagram to compare how their approach to success compared to Sam.
2. What would be your rules for success in life? List at least three rules you think everyone should follow in order to be successful in life.
3. What is an entrepreneur? Sam was a successful entrepreneur. Complete the biography organizer on another successful entrepreneur. (suggestions: Steve Jobs, Bill Gates, Oprah Winfrey, Benjamin Franklin)

SAM WALTON'S TEN RULES FOR SUCCESS

(modified to speak to a young generation)

RULE 1: COMMIT

Commit to your academics. It is your job when you are in school to learn. Education is the key that will unlock the door to your future.

RULE 2: SHARE

Share what you have with others. Be a friend who will share games, experiences, ideas and your time freely.

RULE 3: MOTIVATE

Motivate and encourage your peers to be their best and to meet challenges head on.

RULE 4: COMMUNICATE

Communicate clearly to everyone you encounter. Make eye contact and use your words to say what you mean.

RULE 5: APPRECIATE

Appreciate what others do for you. Demonstrate appreciation for your parents, teachers, coaches, and friends for their influence and help in your life.

RULE 6: CELEBRATE

Celebrate when you succeed! Show the world the trophy, medal or award you have earned and give credit to those who helped you achieve it.

RULE 7: LISTEN

Listen to others so you can learn from them. Be like a sponge soaking in knowledge.

RULE 8: EXCEED

Exceed in your academic, athletic, and artistic pursuits. Set high standards. Don't settle for being average—give your best in everything you do.

RULE 9: CONTROL

Control your time. You only have so many minutes in a day. Use them wisely.

RULE 10: SWIM UPSTREAM

Swim in the opposite direction from the pack mentality. Be a leader, not a follower.

Vocabulary

Authors often use new and interesting vocabulary words. Jot down at least 10 new words as you read the book.

1. ____________________

2. ____________________

3. ____________________

4. ____________________

5. ____________________

6. ____________________

7. ____________________

8. ____________________

9. ____________________

10. ____________________

Find more words? Write them on the back of this sheet.

Digging Deeper with Vocabulary

Choose three of your vocabulary words to work on in depth. Complete the chart below with the three words.

Word:
Sentence in Book where Word is Used:
Definition of Word:
Use the Word in a New Sentence:
Word:
Sentence in Book where Word is Used:
Definition of Word:
Use the Word in a New Sentence:
Word:
Sentence in Book where Word is Used:
Definition of Word:
Use the Word in a New Sentence:

Setting

Setting is important in any story, whether in a fiction book or in someone's actual history. Identify two settings from Sam's life. Then list a minimum of three descriptions for each of the settings.

Setting 1:

Setting 2:

Biography Final Product Choice Menu

Select __________ of the following choices to create a final product to demonstrate your understanding of Young Sam Walton. The product must be completed by:

______________________ .

Imagine that you could have an interview with Sam Walton. Create a list of five questions you would ask him. Tell why the answers to the questions are important to you.
Use your technology skills to tell about Sam's life by creating an IMovie, Power Point, or Google Slideshow.
Design a new book jacket for the book. It will need a full color cover, a three-paragraph summary in the front flap, author biography in the back flap, and two reviews on the back cover.
Write a letter to a famous person recommending the book. Why would they be interested in reading it? Give at least three reasons to persuade them to read the book. Use the friendly letter format.
Create a new title for the book. Give three reasons explaining why you chose that title.

Biography Final Product Scoring Rubric

Name: ______________________ Product Selected: ______________________

Category/Comments	Score
Completion	
Effort	
Content	
Conventions (spelling, grammar, punctuation, capitalization)	
Neatness	

Compare and Contrast

Compare and Contrast yourself to young Sam. In the left circle write five or more descriptions of Sam. In the right circle write five or more descriptions of yourself. Where the circles join, write 3-5 descriptions of how you are similar.

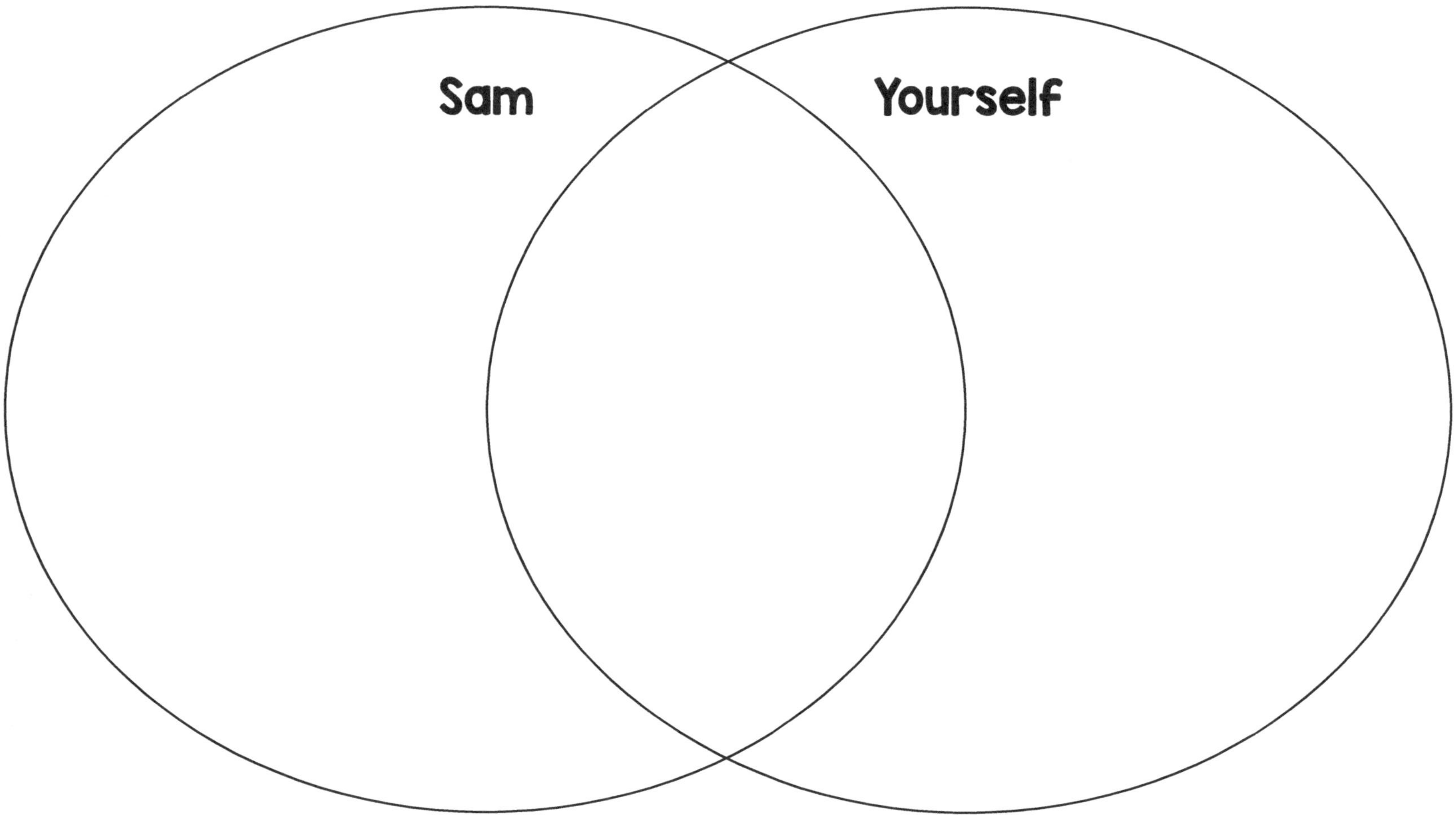

STEM NOTES

The acronym STEM represents the following: Science, Technology, Engineering, and Math. For the purpose of the STEM challenges with this book, you may keep the following in mind:

Science: any of the branches of natural or physical science.

Technology: for the purpose of STEM, technology is anything man made (even a pencil!).

Engineering: with students, this has everything to do with teaching them how to use an identified process to solve problems.

Math: with STEM this uses the language of numbers, symbols, quantities and even non-standard units of measure.

You can search online and find any number of engineering design process steps or loops to guide your students.

1. Give students a real world problem to be solved.
2. Have students imagine, think, or brainstorm solutions with their team.
3. After time has been allowed for brainstorming, have the student(s) select one solution to build.
4. Build! Give students time to build their intended solution. Don't give them ideas; continue to ask students how they can solve the problem with the materials given.
5. Experiment, test, evaluate: Encourage students to test what they are building and let them know it is OK for them to make changes as they build. That is part of the engineering process: realizing they need to adjust.
6. Share results, ask how it could be improved: This step sometimes lends itself to gallery walks to allow students to see how others solved the same problem but in a different way. Even if the build was successful, have students reflect on the process so they can determine improvements in their process the next time.

Gather the Eggs

Young Sam has lost the basket he uses to gather the eggs. The chickens typically lay at least 8 eggs a day. Using the materials provided, design a container he can use to carry eight eggs into the farm house. Your teacher will mark the distance you must travel on the floor.

Materials:

- ✓ 8 ping pong balls
- ✓ 3-12 inch pieces of masking tape
- ✓ 12-pipe cleaners
- ✓ 8-craft sticks
- ✓ 12-drinking straws
- ✓ 1-sheet computer paper
- ✓ Scissors

Build the Bridge

Engineers are building a new bridge on Highway 63. Help them design and build a beam bridge that will span the river so the Walton family can travel safely to Columbia, Missouri.

Be sure to review and use the engineering design loop.

Requirements:

- ✓ The river you are spanning is 7 inches wide.
- ✓ Your bridge must support a minimum weight that your teacher will determine.
- ✓ The support beams may have no more than 3 one-inch pieces of tape attaching them to the table top.
- ✓ You do not have to use all the materials.

Materials:

- ✓ 2 sheets cardstock
- ✓ 2 sheets computer paper
- ✓ Scissors
- ✓ Masking tape: 24 inches maximum
- ✓ Minimum weight item(s)

Challenge Tips and Helpful Links:

Tips for STEM Challenges

GATHER THE EGGS:

I recommend you require students to be able to carry the eggs a distance of twelve feet.

BUILD THE BRIDGE:

For this challenge, you can have students measure the 7 inches for the river with a ruler and mark the edges with masking tape on their workspace. Or you can cut 7-inch wide strips of blue construction paper for them to use to represent the river.

Remind students that the support beams should not be placed in the water.

Use whatever you have readily available for the weight to be supported. You can use pennies, teddy bear counters or even a paperback book that the bridge must support. If you use smaller items for the weight you may want to provide a cupcake liner to represent the Walton car and to hold the pennies or bear counters.

****

MIT Video explaining bridges: https://youtu.be/IBP7739C83s

Types of engineers by SciShow Kids:

https://www.youtube.com/watch?v=D9I35Rqo04E

Think Like an Engineer #1 by SciShow Kids:

https://youtu.be/RM04n0-QtNo

Think Like an Engineer #2 by SciShow Kids:

https://youtu.be/zrAI6JQ3sb4

PBS Kids Video walking through the engineering design loop:

http://pbskids.org/designsquad/video/kid-engineer-design-process/

Want to show videos without advertisements and pop-ups? Use viewpure.com to purify the videos you show to your students.

Copy and paste the URL and click purify. View Pure will block the ads and promotions from popping up.

http://viewpure.com/

Biography Graphic Organizer

Early Life Facts:

1.

2.

3.

Famous for:

1.

2.

3.

Born: ________

Died: ________

Extra Facts:

1.

2.

3.

Name 3 important dates and tell why they are important:

1.

2.

3.

Student Name: ______________________________

What was this individual like as a child? What were his or her goals and dreams?

Why is it important to learn about this individual?

Name:

Born:

Died:

List five fast facts about the individual.

1.

2.

3.

4.

5.

List important dates from the individual's life and tell why the dates are important.